OFFICIAL SOUVENIR
WORLD'S FAIR
ST. LOUIS
1904

KENTUCKY STATE BUILDING. *Oct 18*

UNITED STATES GOVERNMENT BUILDING (LOUISIANA PURCHASE EXPOSITION.)

OFFICIAL SOUVENIR
POST CARD

VARIED INDUSTRIES BUILDING.

FESTIVAL HALL AND CASCADES, WORLD'S FAIR 1904, ST. LOUIS, MO.

Official Souvenir
World's Fair
St. Louis
1904

WASHINGTON STATE BUILDING.

PALACE OF TRANSPORTATION
525 BY 1,300 FEET, COVERING OVER FIFTEEN ACRES.

WORLDS FAIR
ST. Louis Mo.
1904

PALACE OF MANUFACTURES.
525 BY 1300 FEET. AREA IN ACRES.

Official Souvenir
World's Fair
St. Louis
1904

This book is dedicated to my marathon-running-addicted family: My dad, who has run seventeen marathons; my sister Bridget, who is the fastest marathoner I know; cousin Laura, who is well on her way to beating my dad's record; cousin Michael, who likes to push himself to the limit and then relax for the rest of the weekend; and little sister Kaila, a self-proclaimed "jack of all trades and master of none." The exception is my mom, who isn't addicted to long distance running and only accidentally ran seventeen miles once when she went on a three-mile run, got lost, and kept running until she made her way home. Overzealous runs should always get "a mention."

Note: All quotations are from newspapers and reports of the time. See bibliography for references.

SIMON & SCHUSTER BOOKS FOR YOUNG READERS • An imprint of Simon & Schuster Children's Publishing Division • 1230 Avenue of the Americas, New York, New York 10020 • Copyright © 2016 by Meghan McCarthy • All rights reserved, including the right of reproduction in whole or in part in any form. • SIMON & SCHUSTER BOOKS FOR YOUNG READERS is a trademark of Simon & Schuster, Inc. • For information about special discounts for bulk purchases, please contact Simon & Schuster Special Sales at 1-866-506-1949 or business@simonandschuster.com. • The Simon & Schuster Speakers Bureau can bring authors to your live event. For more information or to book an event, contact the Simon & Schuster Speakers Bureau at 1-866-248-3049 or visit our website at www.simonspeakers.com. • Book design by Chloë Foglia • The text for this book is set in Wilke. • The illustrations for this book are rendered in acrylic. • Manufactured in China • 1215 SCP • 10 9 8 7 6 5 4 3 2 1 • Library of Congress Cataloging-in-Publication Data • McCarthy, Meghan. • The wildest race ever : the story of the 1904 Olympic marathon / Meghan McCarthy ; illustrated by Meghan McCarthy . • pages cm • Summary: "The exciting and bizarre true story of the 1904 Olympic marathon, which took place at the St. Louis World's Fair."—Provided by publisher. • ISBN 978-1-4814-0639-0 (hardback) — ISBN 978-1-4814-0640-6 (eBook) • 1. Marathon running—History—Juvenile literature. 2. Olympics—History—Juvenile literature. 3. Olympic Games (3rd : 1904 : Saint Louis, Mo.)—Juvenile literature. I. Title. • GV1065.M43 2016 • 796.42'5209041—dc23 • 2015004822

first edition

THE WILDEST RACE EVER

THE STORY OF THE 1904 OLYMPIC MARATHON

Meghan McCarthy

A Paula Wiseman Book

Simon & Schuster Books for Young Readers

NEW YORK   LONDON   TORONTO   SYDNEY   NEW DELHI

The first Olympic marathon held in America happened on August 30, 1904, in Saint Louis, Missouri. It was part of the World's Fair exhibition. At the World's Fair many people experienced their first hot dog, first Dr Pepper, first ice-cream cone, and first Olympics!

Severe rainstorms rolled in several days before the race. A local newspaper reported, "An automobile party went over the route yesterday and the roads were found to be almost entirely washed away." Officials mapped out a new course. Unfortunately, the new course was more difficult.

Although forty-one runners had signed up to run, only thirty-two started on the day of the race. These are some of the runners:

FRED LORZ—#31
AMERICAN
Lorz was a Boston bricklayer who trained at night, after he finished his day's work. He qualified by running a five-mile race.

FELIX CARVAJAL—#3
CUBAN
Carvajal was a mailman from Cuba. One newspaper described him as a "little fellow with black snappy eyes." He arrived wearing long pants, a long-sleeved shirt, and work shoes. It seems that at some point his shirt got cut. Was this so he could run better?

JOHN LORDEN—#UNKNOWN
AMERICAN
Lorden was the winner of the 1903 Boston Marathon. During training Lorden said, "I am in great condition this year. Never felt better in my life."

SAM MELLOR—#10
AMERICAN
Mellor was the winner of the 1902 Boston Marathon and the Pan-American Exposition. The *Brooklyn Daily Eagle* called "Little Sammy" a "New York Boy," as he represented New York.

ARTHUR NEWTON—#12
AMERICAN
From New York City, Newton placed fifth in the Paris Olympics in 1900.

ALBERT COREY—#7
FRENCH
Corey was French but ran wearing the Chicago Athletic Association colors. Corey was a strikebreaker who worked in stockyards. A strikebreaker is someone who works while other workers are on strike. (Most workers are not fond of strikebreakers.)

WILLIAM GARCIA—#UNKNOWN
AMERICAN
Garcia, a carpenter, was "nearly six feet tall . . . with shapely, slender legs drawn down like a deer's at the ankles," reported the *San Francisco Chronicle*. "The greatest long-distance runner on the Pacific Coast."

JAN MASHIANI—#36
LEN TAU—#35
SOUTH AFRICAN
Mashiani and Tau were employees of the World's Fair. They had carried messages during the Boer War of the late 1800s, and were known for running long distances without stopping.

THOMAS HICKS—#20
AMERICAN,
BORN IN ENGLAND
Hicks thought he was prepared but had trained on flat ground. He was not prepared for all the hills in Saint Louis. Was Hicks in trouble?

There were eleven additional runners from the United States, including the first American Indian to run in the Olympic Games, who was from the Seneca Nation. There was also another South African, a runner from Newfoundland (now part of Canada), and nine representing Greece.

People weren't sure who would win.

It was ninety degrees out on the day of the 24.85-mile marathon. (Marathons today are 26.2 miles.) Thousands of people sat on risers while anxiously awaiting the start of the race. . . .

The runners put one foot forward in ready position. Was anyone nervous? Were they ready to run?

"Gentlemen, I wish you a speedy journey and may the best man win!" announced the president of the fair. The runners were packed tightly at the starting line, waiting for the starting pistol to fire.

It was a bit past three in the afternoon when . . . *POW!* The gun went off and the race was on!

The runners rounded the stadium. Some ran harder than others. Marathons were invented in ancient Greece, but the Greek runners did not amaze spectators on this particular day. "The nine men ran bunched, and with great shocks of curly hair," wrote one reporter, and were "more interested in personal appearance than covering ground."

One runner who was interested in covering ground was American
Fred Lorz. He took off like a bullet and was in first place!

After lapping five times around the stadium, the runners hit the hilly dirt road. Race judges, doctors, and reporters followed in cars. Bicycles also followed. All the wheels spinning around and around in the dirt sent dust clouds into the air. The runners could hardly breathe!

Even though John Lorden was a champion in Boston, he was not looking like one in Saint Louis. He began vomiting in the first mile!

It was a sweltering hot day, and water was only offered to the runners from a water tower at mile six and from a well at mile twelve. Some of the lucky runners had a trainer follow them by car with something to eat and drink. But many didn't. What's worse was that contaminated water made some of the runners ill.

Two miles into the race, Americans, including Sam Mellor and Fred Lorz, were fighting for position. Lorden got cramps and was out of the race. Thomas Hicks was somewhat behind but continued to chug along.

At about mile nine, Lorz was overcome with cramps. He stopped running, got into an automobile, and drove off. Was that the end of Lorz?

Albert Corey and William Garcia were neck and neck.

Although Hicks had been behind, he was catching up!

"The streets were inches deep in dust," Hicks's trainer remarked, "and every time an auto passed it raised enough dust to obscure the vision of the runners and choke them."

Felix Carvajal ran tirelessly. Until, of course, he didn't. Anytime people cheered for the five-foot-tall Cuban, he jogged up to them and chatted, wishing to practice his English. Then he tipped his hat good day. This slowed him down—by a lot.

When Carvajal spotted men eating peaches in an automobile, he couldn't resist temptation. After they refused to give him the peaches, he snatched a few "playfully," as one reporter described, and ran on, eating them as he went.

Two other men took the lead: Arthur Newton and Mellor. But . . . not for long. Soon Mellor began to walk. Hicks finally caught up and joined Newton in the lead. Then Mellor began running again and passed Newton and Hicks! Who would win? It was Mellor . . . then Newton . . . then Hicks! The race was on!

Meanwhile . . . South African Len Tau lost much time when he was chased a mile off course by an angry dog!

Meanwhile . . . Carvajal had been making good time, despite wearing street clothes and despite the fact that he kept pausing to chat with passersby to practice his English. His downfall, however, say some accounts, was when he came upon an apple orchard. He couldn't help but stop to eat some delicious juicy apples! He was hungry!

Meanwhile . . . Mellor was in the lead but was experiencing severe cramping. He was running slower . . . and slower . . . and slower! The other men were gaining! Mellor slowed to a walk. He, too, was out of the race.

Hicks was still going, but by mile ten he was begging for water. His trainers refused to give him any. Instead, they gave him strychnine. Strychnine is a kind of rat poison! It was the early 1900s, and science wasn't as advanced. Hicks's trainers thought giving him this was a good thing to do. They thought it would make him run faster! The trainers combined the rat poison with an egg white. What an odd combination. Would this help Hicks or hurt him?

Meanwhile . . . a doctor who was driving alongside the racers to help those in need of medical attention soon found himself in need of his own! His automobile plummeted down a thirty-foot embankment. The doctor and another man inside the auto were rescued and taken to the hospital. Newspapers reported that the men would survive.

Meanwhile . . . Lorz appeared out of the dust. He'd passed Hicks and the other runners. It was reported that Lorz ran "the last lap of the track like a steam engine." He flew through the tape and was declared the winner. "An American has won!" people shouted. The crowd roared.

Just then someone demanded that the ceremony be stopped! Lorz cheated! The crowd went from cheers to boos. Lorz claimed it was a joke. He said he was feeling better, so he ran the rest of the way. The race committee said this was unacceptable and decided to ban Lorz "for life" from competing.

Meanwhile . . . Hicks was struggling. He was only two miles from the finish when he came upon a large hill. He began to walk. Just as soon as he did, cheers from the crowd sounded. This perked Hicks up. He began to run once more. Perhaps there was hope!

His trainers gave him another mixture of strychnine and an egg white. "Over the last two miles of the road," wrote his trainer Charles Lucas, "Hicks was running mechanically, his arms appeared as weights well tied down; he could scarcely lift his legs."

Do you think giving Hicks more strychnine was a good idea?

Things got worse for Hicks. He thought he had twenty miles to go instead of a mile! Perhaps it was the poison. He began begging for food and water, and then to lie down. When a reporter asked how he was doing, he stated, "I want something to eat as soon as I get there. I'm nearly starved." Hicks asked for water, but was given a warm sponge bath instead.

Every runner in the 1904 marathon accomplished something huge. They weren't afraid to attempt a long and almost impossible race. They all ran side by side, competitors from different parts of the globe. That's what the Olympics and marathon running is all about!

The Marathon Runners

Felix Carvajal "is one of the most interesting characters in the marathon business," one reporter wrote. There are differing accounts of how Carvajal arrived at the Olympic games in 1904. One newspaper reported that he arrived in Santiago and "asked the ruler of the city for funds to take him to St. Louis and was turned down." After being turned away, Carvajal "kept going in the hot sun and a great crowd gathered. A purse was raised and the little man came to the United States."

Another paper described Carvajal this way: "Yes, he was undoubtedly crazy." This newspaper then explained why Carvajal kept stopping along the marathon route to eat: "Carvajal needed something to eat on the way. The Cuban came to St. Louis. For three days he didn't have a bite of food." I found another, more elaborate account that claimed that Carvajal had made a pit stop in New Orleans and gambled his money away. By the time he made it to the finish line, reported this paper, Carvajal was starving.

Finishing fourth was not the end of Carvajal. Apparently, he was scheduled to run a marathon in Athens, Greece. He boarded a ship and arrived in Italy but never appeared in Athens. One paper said that Carvajal's obituary was printed in Cuban newspapers. Miraculously, Carvajal turned up in Havana. An agent who went by the name of Big Jim was vacationing in Cuba and discovered Carvajal. A paper said that Big Jim "dug up a live one." Carvajal was "signed" and became a professional runner.

For training purposes Carvajal strapped bells around his waist and timed his pace by the jingle. His trainer said that while in Cuba, Carvajal ran from town to town "posing as a celebrity and would bring a car horn with him and squeeze the honk-honk bulb until a crowd collected."

Credit: Missouri History Museum, Saint Louis

Hicks after the victory

As papers suggested, now that Carvajal was under contract, he would be going back to the States: "As this kind of racing is all the rage right now, there is little doubt but that Carvajal will have plenty of engagements."

Albert Corey continued running. "[Thomas Hicks] fainted at the tape, while Corey finished waving and smiling to his friends." After completing the 1904 marathon as promised, Corey made a go at running longer distances. Ultramarathons are becoming popular today, with people participating in five-day races, running from twenty-five to fifty miles per day. Corey was definitely ahead of his time! In 1905 he attempted to beat a one-hundred-mile running record but failed. He ran 23:10. His slow time was said to be due to muddy conditions as he "finished with a great burst of speed." Two years later a news headline read: ONE HUNDRED MILE RECORD SHATTERED BY ALBERT L. COREY. Corey successfully beat the record and ran one hundred miles in 18:33.

Thomas Hicks insisted that he never wanted to race again. He said the 1904 Olympic marathon was the worst race ever. No wonder! An article in *New Scientist* talked about Hicks's use of strychnine. It said, "Strychnine interferes with the neurotransmitter glycine, triggering a frenzy of neuronal activity in the spinal cord and muscles." Paul Dargan, a toxicologist at the National Poisons Information Service in London, was quoted as saying, "Strychnine would definitely not be associated with any performance enhancement. Strychnine makes all the muscles fire at once, in a chaotic fashion rather than in the ordered way you need for running. It decreases muscle efficiency and that's not a positive thing for an athlete." There is no mention of Hicks using strychnine again.

"There seemed to be little interest on the part of the public in the games," wrote the *San Francisco Chronicle*. There are scenes where there is not an observer in sight. Crowds can be seen at the starting line, sitting in the bleachers, but they are not at all full. It's clear that people's interests were elsewhere. This may have been due, in part, to the decision to combine the 1904 Olympics, originally scheduled to be held in Chicago that same year, with the World's Fair. Another problem may have been that, without the use of a television, a marathon is not much of a spectator sport. Regardless, many missed quite a race.

At the 1904 World's Fair

Picture miles of tall white-columned buildings with state and country flags flying atop each, expansive rectangular blue pools of water enticing visitors to take gondola rides, and marble statues of animals and figures. There were fountains, neatly trimmed hedges, mowed lawns, and many colorful flowers. There was so much to see it was said it would take months to get through it all. There was a palace of transportation, agriculture, liberal arts, electricity, machinery, education, and more. Even though flight wasn't perfected yet, people witnessed inventors attempting to get their flying machines off the ground! Some crashed into the bushes, but a few made it into the air. There were competitions to see how long an airship could stay in flight. The World's Fair was the perfect venue to show off new creations.

At the Pike

People liked going to the Pike because it offered a carnival aspect to the fair. There was something for everyone, from sideshows to rides. In the Japanese section spectators observed a man carving an image out of a single grain of rice.

Visitors entered realistic depictions of the Arctic containing white lands full of towering icelike glaciers. At the Pike there was also a replica of a giant ship, with walkways that jostled to imitate the motion of the sea.

Carl Hagenbeck's Zoological Paradise featured a trained zebra, trained polar bears and lions, performing seals that balanced balls on their noses, and a trainer who dined at a table with at least four large tigers. In one photo there is a grassy lawn where children are riding on giant tortoises while guiding them with what appear to be sticks of lettuce.

When asked about the Pike, the oldest Roosevelt boy said, "Ain't it bully," which loosely translates to "Awesome!" According to the *Los Angeles Times*, the president's daughter Alice Roosevelt visited the Pike incognito and made her way through the Pike galloping on the back of a donkey.

One of the most unique aspects of the fair was the "living exhibits," which were peoples from different countries who were invited to live at the World's Fair. Having people on display may seem cringeworthy, but it seemed in part like an honest attempt to relate to other cultures. Of course, there was a voyeuristic quality to it much like how reality TV is today.

ILLINOIS STATE BLDG.

Select Bibliography

Boston Daily Globe. "Cambridge Boy Won Marathon: Hicks Beat 30 Good Men, Time Slow 3h 28m." August 31, 1904.

Chicago Inter Ocean. "The 'Man Killing' Marathon Race." September 9, 1904.

Cincinnati Enquirer. "Handicapped by Huge Moustache He Covered 26 Miles, After Going Hungry for Three Days." March 31, 1906.

Jeffersonian Gazette (Lawrence, KS). "Over a 30-Foot Embankment." August 31, 1904.

Lucas, Charles J. P. *The Olympic Games, 1904.* Saint Louis: Woodward & Tieran, 1905.

McConaughy, J. "Hicks, An American, Winner and Hero of Marathon Race." *Saint Louis Post-Dispatch*, August 31, 1904.

New York Evening World. "Cuban Runner Carvajal Comes to Life." April 11, 1907.

Pain, Stephanie. "Marathon Madness." *New Scientist.* August 13, 2014.

Saint Louis Post-Dispatch. "Race: New Route, Necessitated by Washouts, Is One of the Hardest Ever Faced." August 24, 1904.

San Francisco Chronicle. "Garcia to Run in Marathon: Olympic Club's Crack Distance Man To . . ." August 12, 1904.

San Francisco Chronicle. "Hicks of Harvard, Wins the Marathon: American Long Distance Runner . . ." August 31, 1904.

Van Der Merwe, Floris J.G. "Africa's First Encounter with the Olympic Games In . . . 1904." *Journal of Olympic History* (September 1999): 29–34.

Washington Post. "Vanderbilts Give Dinner in Honor of Miss Roosevelt." August 30, 1904.

Washington Times. "Foreigners Gave Ludicrous Show." August 31, 1904.

—— For the full bibliography, please go to ——
meghan-mccarthy.com/wildestrace_bibliography.html.

PALACE OF VARIED INDUSTRIES
525 BY 1240 FEET. COST $800,000
APPROXIMATE AREA 14 ACRES.

WORLDS FAIR
St. Louis Mo.
1904

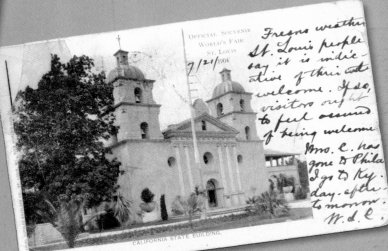

OFFICIAL SOUVENIR
WORLD'S FAIR
ST. LOUIS

CALIFORNIA STATE BUILDING.

PALACE OF MINES AND METALLURGY
525 BY 750 FEET. AREA 9 ACRES. COST $502,000

WORLDS FAIR
St. Louis Mo.
1904

PALACE OF EDUCATION AND SOCIAL ECONOMY.
525 FEET BY AN AVERAGE OF 600 FEET. AREA 7 ACRES. COST $319,000

PALACE OF LIBERAL ARTS.
525 BY 750 FEET. COST $480,000

WORLDS FAIR
St. Louis Mo.
1904

Hæss Envelope Co. St. Louis, America.

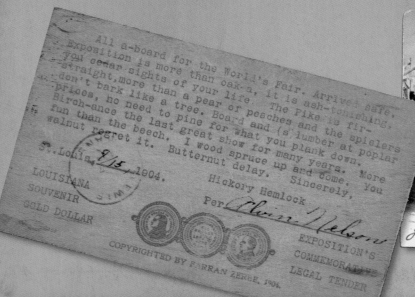

All a-board for the World's Fair. Arrived safe.
Exposition is more than oak-a, it is ash-tonishing.
You cedar sights of your life. The Pike is fir-
straight, more than a pear of peaches and the spielers
don't bark like a tree. Board and (s'lumber at poplar
prices, no need to pine for what you plank down.
Birch-ance the last great show for many years. More
fun than the beech. I wood spruce up ard come. You
walnut regret it. Butternut delay. Sincerely,
Hickory Hemlock
St. Louis, 9/15, 1904.   Per Elvin Nelson

LOUISIANA
SOUVENIR
GOLD DOLLAR

COPYRIGHTED BY FARRAN ZERBE, 1904.

EXPOSITION'S
COMMEMORATIVE
LEGAL TENDER

St. Louis Worlds Fair 1904   Statuary on swinging Columns
Curt Teich & Co., Chicago and St. Louis.   No. 101